I appreciate all the Support you've given, and look forward to growing our friendship.

YOUR NAKED BRAND

THE GUIDE TO BUILDING YOUR BRANDED EMPIRE

By Basim Mirza

Edited by Zacharie Weingarten

Your Naked Brand: The Guide to Building Your Branded Empire

ISBN 10: 0984846271

ISBN 13: 978-0-9848462-7-6

Cover photo by Ahmed Nizam.

"Your name, reputation and brand – in the eyes of others – is your most valuable asset, and this book shows you how to build and maintain it through life."

Brian Tracy – Author, *Unlimited Sales Success*

"Basim is one of those people who works magic. He understands the power of networking, strategy, and social media to turn any idea into a successful product. He can turn an idea into pure gold."

Tash Jefferies, Best Selling Author of *The Little Book of Green Minutes*

"A powerful read with great insights. Basim Mirza uses real life experiences to demonstrate powerful tools. This step by step guide will turn your personal brand into a valuable personal asset."

Ray Brooks, Angel Investor, Former U.N. Advisor

"Basim is a force with experience and intuition second to none. Learning from his techniques would be a true blessing to anyone willing to grow the seeds that he provides. As a mentor and an author, I know that a personal brand is everything and is the key to long-lasting, substantial results for your business and for your legacy. I highly recommend this book if you're looking for the keys to building your empire!"

Melyssa Moniz, Author of *Live Your Passion* and *Key Questions to Help You Identify and Create Your Success*

"Basim's book is definitely a must read AND Basim himself is a must follow! If you're looking to succinctly brand yourself in today's media-rich environ, Basim Mirza provides a successful system to help us make lasting impressions about YOU. Why wait? Start now!"

Tom Supra, Professor, School of Business, Arts, and Design, George Brown College

"Basim has hit the mark! His strategies are the key ingredients for anyone looking to land their dream opportunity"

Kasia, Content Marketer at Udemy

"Basim lays out a comprehensive guide to effective storytelling that captures the imaginations of fans, clients, and future business partners. Must read for anyone looking to become a notable thought leader in their industry."

The Food Story Team

"Brilliant! This book is a game changer! Basim is a breakthrough leader in his field, his insights are innovative and will inspire future leaders for many years to come."

Beau Pinto, Online Marketing Expert and Entrepreneur

As a Financial Adviser who values second and third degree networking, this book is an asset for anyone looking to attract incredible opportunities.

Joseph Miniaci, Top Producing Financial Consultant

“Basim’s diverse background, coupled with collabrative leadership is exactly what our young entreprenuers need. A great model for corporate and academic success.”

Grant Larsen, Growth Consultant

“Aside from being able to captivate an audience, Basim has the ability to cover an extremely wide spectrum of topics in the realm of Personal Branding while being able to call upon his own experiences and expertise to speak about them specifically as well.”

Kamil Shafiq, Social Media and Marketing Expert

“Basim’s theory “you are your personal brand” is the new code for how business works. He can help you bridge the gap between where you are, and where you want to be.”

Nawar Nory, President of Help Elves & CEO of CETsy

“Your Naked Brand is quite the page turner for prospective entrepreneurs who are looking to create, optimize and transform their personal branding efforts into a value-driven lifestyle. Worth the read, thanks for your insights Mr. Mirza!”

Ahmed Nizam, Founder & Creative Director, Nizam Photography

Dedicated To

The legacy and spirit of Napoleon Hill
(1883-1970).

Contents

Chapter 1
Starting From Scratch

Your personal brand is applicable in all walks of life, whether you're a working professional, an entrepreneur, or even if you're unemployed. The proven strategies I share in this guide will turn your passions into a dream come true. Building your personal brand will require a lot of work. My proven tools and strategies can be used to build your personal brand up from the core. You will have to dig deep and understand where your passions are rooted. You will have to understand what makes you the person you are today. The tools and strategies I share with you in this guide will catapult you to new levels immediately. If you apply everything in this guide, you will have a solid foundation for bringing your personal brand to fruition. Social media can help you cultivate the right relationships, build authentic networks, and find huge opportunities. However, it's just a tool, and the traditional ways of business and personal development are still as effective as ever. The online tools we have today accelerate the process of building a personal brand. The end goal is to monetize and build profit channels to serve your own interests. Through my proven process for building an effective personal brand, you will learn how to build profitable avenues for yourself. Whether it's about positioning yourself for a promotion within your company, getting clients to pay you for your

> THE TRADITIONAL WAYS OF BUSINESS AND PERSONAL DEVELOPMENT ARE STILL AS EFFECTIVE AS EVER

time, or using your personal brand to create online revenue streams, this book will guide you towards your career goals by using simple yet powerful techniques. Through my system, you will reap the benefits of a strong personal brand right away. I've broken down personal branding into simple terms and have developed a process that I am confident is easy to follow. I want you to succeed. Let's execute and break new barriers together.

You may have already made multiple efforts towards building your personal brand, or perhaps this is your first time. One way or another, as long as you're prepared to execute, you'll be moving forward. You will be getting the most results from this proven system. I've mentored and lectured thousands of individuals from all walks of life. The methods shown in this book are applicable to anyone at any stage. Personal branding is a process of learning and building. You have to be willing to adapt to the needs of your network. Once you've identified the needs, react with the solutions. By serving those around you, you've already taken the first step towards establishing yourself as an expert. This continual process allows your personal brand to evolve into an asset. You can leverage your personal brand to attract new opportunities. Whether it's a business powerhouse you're looking to build or a

YOU HAVE TO BE WILLING TO ADAPT TO THE NEEDS OF YOUR NETWORK successful career you're looking to establish, your personal brand will support you. I have been blessed to have the opportunity to share my passions with the world, and I am thankful for the amazing influencers that surround me. I'm now at a point in my career where I'm prepared to give back. I'm laying out all the tools, strategies, and processes that have helped me get to where I am today. By applying these methodologies I was able to carry my personal brand to new heights. The right clients started to find me, my speaking and coaching career catapulted. I started to become well established throughout my extensive networks, and became accredited as an expert in my field. Throughout this guide I will be discussing both online and offline strategies. Please don't get discouraged by the complexity of these strategies, I will break it all down for you in simple terms. Making it to the end of this guide will be a great achievement and will have a measurable impact on your personal development. I will do my job by making sure you're able to fully understand the concepts I share with you. The content in this guide will help you cultivate the right relationships, build authentic networks, and find opportunities. This entire book is dedicated to increasing efficiency and reducing costs, which will be reflected in your success and the bottom line of your intended business model. The personal branding strategies I share will nudge you towards fast execution and rapid iteration. My aim is to simplify the process of personal branding and eliminate all the headaches.

You've decided to invest in this book; now reap the full benefit by reading it thoroughly.

Core Values

At many points in my life I felt indecisive. I was unsure of the things that were relevant to what I was doing and felt like I didn't have my priorities set straight. This was a result of me not having fully determined my core values, which reflected on the things that mattered to me the most. Setting my core values not only saved me time, it also motivated me towards fulfilling my definite purpose in life.

Before we dive into all the technical concepts, I feel as if it is important to fully understand how your personal brand will be rooted. Your core values will act as a foundation for everything you do, your passion and work will stem from your personal beliefs. The questions I'm about to ask you are not just any questions; they are questions that will reflect on your character and personality. Thinking enough about this will strengthen the core strength behind your personal brand. When you strip off all the external layers and infrastructure, and your personal brand is naked, your core values are what you're left with. These core values will channel the spiritual message behind your personal brand and will elevate what you've built to new realms. Having a spiritual focus will allow you to channel your energies towards a defined purpose.

Core Questions to Ask Yourself

- Who are your idols?
  Why?
- What motivates you to succeed?
  Why?
- What are your desires?
  Why?

Channeling Passion

Our varieties of thoughts and feelings come from different places and are different for each person. This is the reason why we are all unique and set out for different paths. You have to find your passion; it is the lifeblood of your personal brand. It should feel as if it is a part of you, and is inseparable from your beliefs. Understanding why you are passionate is the best way to start. Only then can you truly understand how to use your passion to build your personal brand. The intensity and build up behind these feelings should urge you to tell the world about your passion. You should be ready to not only embrace it, but also let it become a part of your world. Once you do this, you'll find all the right avenues for your personal brand. Most people just don't know where to start, which is why they end up not taking action at all. If this is your situation right now, I've put together questions to help you kick-start a concept. The model below will help you formulate a general idea of what you are passionate about. Understand that this process will evolve. The key here is to learn and further develop your thinking as you explore these concepts further. With enough persistence your infrastructure will start to piece itself together.

Passion Questions

- What are 3 things you love to do in your spare time?
  Example: Knitting, Sports, and Socializing.
- What are 3 skills you bring to the table?
  Example: Graphic Design, Analytics, and Sales.
- What sort of opportunities do you want?
  Example: I'm looking for a dream career as a graphic design artist.
- How would you describe your ideal "fan"?
  Example: Entrepreneurs and business owners looking for creative design work.

Over the years my content naturally became more defined, and I started moving towards business development. My work evolved into social media and entrepreneurship, and shortly afterward I restructured my services towards personal branding. This move became obvious as soon as I began to notice the value I was delivering to my clients. Through my practices, I had been literally transforming their personal brands and launching them to new heights, the same way I catapulted mine. I felt great because my clients had a genuine need for my services and I was there to satisfy them. Through my example you may notice that I became more focused over time. My business models became more defined, and I felt more confident in the value I was delivering.

Understanding what you like to do in your spare time will help you evaluate the key things that keep you happy and motivated. In fact, this sort of information gives you a sense of where your intrinsic drive (the motivation that stems from passion) comes from. If you're able to channel this through your personal brand, you may never have to work a day in your life. Your thoughts today make you the person you will become tomorrow. Your general skill sets will help you evaluate what sort of value you'll be able to exchange. These are transferrable skills

> YOUR THOUGHTS TODAY MAKE YOU THE PERSON YOU WILL BECOME TOMORROW

at all levels. You can use them wherever you wish. Whether you're working in corporate, running your own business, or involved in a not-for-profit, your skill-sets are adaptable. As you grow as a person and take on life as a journey, your personal brand will correlate with the relationships and opportunities that come to you. Keep in mind that your personal brand is an asset that will grow. The strategies and tools I share with you will build your branded empire. As long as you remain committed to applying the concepts and strategies I share with you, the quality of your relationships and opportunities will grow in conjunction with your input.

Chapter 1 Checklist

1. *Answer the core questions and write them down.*
2. *Answer the passion questions and write them down.*

Chapter 2
Using the Right Tools

To begin to see positive impact right away, we're going to launch your presence on all the appropriate social media platforms. It is important to start building an engaging presence on these platforms right away. This way you'll begin to build your web presence and individuals will start to take notice of your unique personal brand. As you begin to connect with others, you'll also find that your traffic numbers will start to grow.

BUILD YOUR WEB PRESENCE AND INDIVIDUALS WILL START TO TAKE NOTICE OF YOUR UNIQUE PERSONAL BRAND

Infrastructure

The more organized your social media and marketing channels are, the easier it will be to leverage and build traction. First and foremost, you will need to understand the basic social media tools that currently exist and educate yourself on what they bring to the table. I've put together an easy reference table of the applications that I believe to be the most effective. You can always come back and review this table whenever you need guidance. Keep in mind that many of these products will evolve and new ones will come to light. The key here is to understand what you're getting out of your efforts - what the output is. Once you understand this, integrating your brand into future applications will become easier and everything will start to click. Keep in mind that some or even all of these things may seem alien at first. Don't worry; throughout this book I will make use of personal examples. You will be fully equipped. You will succeed.

Social Media as an Accelerator

It is important to initially recognize that all the social media platforms out there are simply tools; they can elevate your results if you use them properly. Rather than being dependant on them to build your brand, it makes more sense to incorporate them into your personal messaging strategy. Recognize the business building aspect of this entire process. There have always been traditional routes to achieve this, even before the internet existed! With that being said, social media is everywhere and it is hard not to get overwhelmed by all the different options. It will be comforting when you identify these tools as accelerators to your current process of building a personal brand. Social media isn't the cause or reason behind your success; it is simply there to give your current strategies a boost.

There are certain tools you can use to help elevate your brand. Understanding their basic functionalities will help you find clients, market to them, and distribute content. These are all different channels to magnify the impact of your word of mouth promotion. It is important to be effective with the tools you use. Managing too many tools could spread you too thin, so take caution. The table below suggests different social media platforms you should use. Come back to this table at your own leisure when you're trying to navigate in the social media realm.

Preferred Social Media Platforms for Personal Branding

Facebook	**Output:** *Text, Links, Photos, Videos.*	**Relevant Utilities:** *Sharing and posting all forms of online content, communicating directly with contacts, sharing information, accessing social networks, planning events, creating fan pages and groups, accessing advanced social searches.*

Facebook[1] has evolved to become the primary social tool to use for online networking. The ability to specify social searches and target specific individuals towards a particular interest is applicable to personal branding. You can tell stories, account your experiences chronologically, and successfully market events to your network. Facebook also makes it easier to communicate through multiple profiles. For example, you could communicate as an individual as well as through a Fan page. Thus you're able to manage multiple brands. The key to using Facebook as a brand-building tool is to build intrinsic value with fellow users by constantly engaging. Using content as a basis for discussion is a great way to accomplish this. Define your success by your ability to create story-telling opportunities.

1 http://www.facebook.com/

LinkedIn	**Output:** *Text, Links, Videos.*	**Relevant Utilities:** *Accessing 2nd degree and 3rd degree networks through mutual links, sharing information, creating professional profiles, embedding video, joining professional groups, receiving and giving recommendations and endorsements, direct mailing and making introductions, performing advanced professional searches.*

LinkedIn[1] is an engagement tool that allows you to connect with others in a professional context. It is built with a business mandate and designed to move you further in your career. This is why it is important to build a solid reputation on LinkedIn. You can quickly put effort towards connecting with everyone you network with, especially contacts in your industry. If you're linked in with clients then you can ask them to write you a recommendation. This builds the credibility of your brand. Once you've built up your LinkedIn profile prominently, you're able to attract visitors to your profile. LinkedIn's premium features allow you to see who has viewed your profile, which helps you identify potential leads for new business relationships.

1 http://www.linkedin.com/

Twitter	**Output:** *Text, Links, Photos.*	**Relevant Utilities:** *Direct limited communication, link shortening, picture embedding, and message distribution.*

Twitter[1] limits every message by 140 characters. This means you have to be straight to the point. Twitter's model is based on influence, which results in additional followers. A follower receives your tweets on his/her wall feed, which can then be retweeted (shared) to reach other networks. The real benefit in all of this is the ability to find influencers and potentially gain their support. Influencers can be industry leaders, celebrities, visionaries, etc. Their support will instantly add credibility to your online profile. Simply having their endorsement is a seed for promotion. It's a success result that you can share with your network. This can result in new followers, as well as the gain of respect within the community. Also, influential users have a high number of followers. If they were to retweet your message to their fan base, you could get further exposure. Your online traffic will increase if an influencer drives visitors to your profile.

1 http://www.twitter.com/

YouTube	**Output:** *Text, Videos, Links.*	**Relevant Utilities:** *Video Publishing, video embedding, traffic building, developing branded channels, back-linking, commenting, direct messaging.*

YouTube[1] has quickly become the number one source for watching and sharing videos. Everyday, users can upload and watch videos of their choice. YouTube is a great avenue for not just personal branding, but monetization as well. The best part about it is you can embed your videos on all other social media platforms as a link or through HTML code. If you're using it to simply upload a video and get it out there, video views may not be your concern. However if you're looking to monetize you should be looking at the views, as this directly reflects how much YouTube pays you through their Partnership Program.

1 http://www.youtube.com/

Google+	**Output:** *Text, Links, Photos, Videos.*	**Relevant Utilities:** *Sharing and posting all forms of online content, video conferencing, publishing online documents, event planning, creating fan pages and groups, performing advanced searches.*

Google+[1] is a tool that has quickly gained respect amongst productive users. It is an innovative platform that networks users within social circles. Through these circles, content is spread in the form of posts. The key benefit for your personal brand comes in how you utilize some of the key features. Google Hangouts is a multi-person video conference platform that allows up to ten people to communicate at once. You're also able to utilize other tools such as Google Drive, which allows you to make notes or create a document. The platform itself endorses creation, which serves as a nest egg for innovative thinkers and visionaries. Google Hangouts allows you to record your conference calls as YouTube videos, and have it broadcasted in the form of video content. You can use this content to promote your overall personal brand, as more people are able to witness your expert dialogues. Google+ becomes very useful when looking to attract certain clients over the internet.

1 http://plus.google.com/

Pinterest	**Output:** *Text, Photos.*	**Relevant Utilities:** *Posting pictures, commenting, sharing.*

Pinterest[1] has become the platform for sharing anything fashion, hobby, design, or art related. It is a social medium that has the ability to distribute feeds to Facebook and Twitter accounts. You have the ability to "re-pin", share, or comment on anything that appeals to you. Through such dialogues you're able to see what's trendy and keep track of your favorite stuff. This adds personality and character to your personal brand because users are able to see your interests on a deeper level. This tool is especially effective if you're looking to end up in the fashion industry, start a clothing store, or even a label. You're able to brand yourself as an expert through your own style, and encourage your clients to check out your regular feeds through Pinterest.

1 http://www.pinterest.com/

Storify	**Output:** *Text, Links, Photos, Videos.*	**Relevant Utilities:** *Story-telling, content creating, publishing, integrating content from multiple feeds*

Storify[1] is a new and upcoming tool. Its not as well known as the other tools, however it certainly holds its weight in value. It is definitely worth mentioning considering the unique features it carries. The platform allows you to integrate elements from different social media profiles and create a story. You're able to pull in Tweets, Facebook posts, Tumblr blogs, etc. You can then put it together to explain a story. This is especially powerful when you're looking to build a story behind your brand. The pieces come together to build a plot, which build intrinsic value for your readers. Your readers then feel more inclined to buy into your brand. You're also able to export these stories in HTML format to other sites, including blogs.

1 http://www.storify.com/

Blogger	**Output:** *Text, Links, Photos, Videos.*	**Relevant Utilities:** *Publishing and posting all forms of online content, back-linking.*

Blogger[1] is a Google product that makes it simple for a user to put out their content through a customizable blog. Every time you post content on Blogger it gets published on the internet. As a result, you increase the search effectiveness of your personal brand. People are able to find you through the content you put out. In fact, you're able to set the hyperlinks back to your main website, which promotes your overall products and services. This is the basis of search engine optimization (SEO). You can position these hyperlinks as specific keywords related to your product. Every time these keywords are clicked, Google recognizes it for your own benefit. Blogger also has its own compensation plan through advertising. I don't recommended that you rely solely on this for your income, as you'll need an incredible amount of views to make this monetization avenue worth your time. Also, by putting up banner ads, you may compromise the aesthetics of your website in return for little payback.

1 http://www.blogger.com/

	Output:	Relevant Utilities:
Tumblr	*Text, Links, Photos, Videos.*	*Publishing and posting all forms of online content, back-linking.*

Tumblr[1] is a more creative output for blogging compared to Blogger. However, this platform gives you access to an entirely different market. By using Tumblr you'll be exposed to a crowd that is typically younger, more tech-savvy, and more socially active online. To increase your search and SEO effectiveness you can duplicate your content onto Tumblr. As mentioned before, there is full integration with Storify as well. Thus it is useful to continually provide updates to your Tumblr to drive more views to other aspects of your online presence.

Building Expertise

Don't let anyone sway you away from the fact that you're an expert. To be an expert at anything, you need to not only feel it, but you need to become the person you want to be. You need to act, dress, and behave exactly like the kind of person you aspire to be. To get to that next stage it's absolutely a matter of immersing yourself in your vision. When considering how to make the best use of social media and online strategies, you'll have to consider the same approach. People should recognize you as an expert, and attach your name to the expertise you've built up.

1 http://www.tumblr.com/

Defined Purpose

It doesn't hurt to explore new and different areas of interest. However, in the grand scheme of things you should be able to narrow it all down. You may end up building on two or three areas of interest and eventually channel it all into one focus. This is where it will be useful to identify some sort of defined purpose, even if it does evolve in the future. Your defined purpose will encourage you to stay on point with what you're trying to accomplish and you'll always have a constant reminder of where you have to go. Your defined purpose acts like a destination. In order for you to get there you need to look ahead at where you're going.

My Defined Purpose Example:

"I help career and business focused individuals understand the growth potential of their networks."

A defined purpose will keep you on point, and will act as your personal mission statement. Looking at it every day will help you stay engaged with your overall purpose. Your lifestyle will naturally begin to support your defined purpose and, eventually, you'll begin to attract the right opportunities at the right time.

Exposure

Build a habit of introducing yourself as a guru, and tie it in with your passion. This helps brand you as an expert in your preferred space. This will also give you a purpose and allow you to add value in other people's lives. When you do this enough times, you will not only get more comfortable with it, you'll start to see opportunities and doors will start to open for you. When you see everyone around you tweeting and using social media extensively, it becomes difficult to differentiate yourself individually. If this is the case, you need to increase the quality of your content. There has to be meaning behind what you write, blog, or even tweet. Understanding your vision will help you build a purpose behind all the content you send out. The best way to capture new audiences with your content is to make them feel confident in your abilities. Show them the results and how those results are having a positive impact on your life.

Chapter 2 Checklist

1. *Create an account for all social media applications that you feel will be useful to your personal branding efforts.*

2. *Introduce yourself on the tools you haven't yet explored.*

Chapter 3

Blog Integration and Landing Pages

Setting up landing pages and blog sites gives you a web presence that helps people find you through web search engines. When you build additional portals, you're adding to your online presence and building new links. Your presence on the web is reflective of your traffic growth. Keep in mind that this chapter will be a different approach to link-building than Chapter 4, which goes into depth about building a proper website. If you don't have a website up yet, then you should at least follow through on the approaches described in this chapter. This way you'll be able to direct people to relevant web pages on the internet. Having a combination of a blog and a great landing page will enhance your credibility on the web.

YOUR PRESENCE ON THE WEB IS REFLECTIVE OF YOUR TRAFFIC GROWTH

Blogging Content

My blog http://www.basim.ca has delivered exceptional value towards helping me build my personal brand. As more people started following it regularly, I became recognized as an expert. I continually defined new paths for myself in the business world, and constantly found profitable opportunities. My blog helped me maintain rapport with important relationships and partners, which in turn increased my conversions for business deals.

A blog in its true essence is a channel for all of your content. This can range from writing knowledgeable articles to posting videos you like or have produced. Your content attracts the right followers, which you can eventually direct towards your monetization channels. The search engines make sure your content is traceable. However, it is on you to make sure the right content is always on your site. I've already mentioned in the previous chapter that you can use platforms like Blogger and Tumblr to get started right away. Both of these tools are highly intuitive and easy to use. You'll get a free sub-domain from them to use. You also have the option to host your blog under a direct domain.[1] This can help create a good impression for your users. The next chapter has instructions on how to buy a domain and point it to your website. The same instructions can be applied to getting your blog linked up as well.

Landing Pages and New Traffic

Creating a landing page is not as complicated as it sounds. A landing page is simply the concept of having a web page on the internet for your users to learn more about you. There are services out there that allow you to create landing pages, and have your entire social media and online portfolio consolidated in one place. AboutMe[2] is a service that allows you to do this instantly. I've footnoted on this page my profile

1 Example: http://www.basim.ca/

2 http://www.about.me/

as an example. Take a look to help you understand how to get your page up and running. It is simple, easy, and highly effective. Your presence will grow and external networks will start paying attention to what you're saying and producing on the internet.

Having multiple landing pages to represent different products and services helped me simplify complex business infrastructures. If you want a target prospect to focus on a specific product or service, you direct them to a landing page. This was why I was motivated to build a process that helped me create multiple landing pages at a rapid rate. This habit turned into a science, and turned out to be a great way to carve different niches. The next chapter will help guide you through this process and master the art of web creation.

Chapter 4
Overnight Website™

I've put together a step by step process to have your website up and running overnight. I'm not kidding, this is for real. My methods will show you exactly how to build a website overnight. You'll have your ".com" up and running on a professional and clean looking website within hours. Best of all, your costs will be less than $10 per month and editing your new website's content will be a piece of cake. Most people get agitated with having to rely on their web developer to make the changes needed, which can be both time consuming and expensive. Once you're comfortable with this process you'll be able to create landing pages on the fly. If you have a new product release you'll be able to point a specific domain to the relevant site. This is a very innovative approach towards promoting new releases.

Having a website is important because it allows your prospective clients and business partners to find you easily. A website will also add to your credibility and you'll find people will feel more inclined to have a discussion with you. Your prospects need a place where they can find out all the information they need to know. It doesn't have to be a company website; you can have one made under your personal name. A website builds your presence on the internet and helps you get recognized by Google's search engine. If your budget is limited because you're just starting out, this is the way to go. My process will reward you with a proper website that is effective and helps you

A WEBSITE BUILDS YOUR PRESENCE ON THE INTERNET

execute your personal brand. On top of all this the costs will be minimal and you'll have the flexibility and freedom to change the content whenever you want.

Buying a Domain

The first step in getting a website set up is to choose a domain URL that makes sense for your brand. If you're positioning yourself as an expert then your name may make sense; just make sure your name isn't hard to spell. Domains should be simple and spelt correctly. You can have a domain name that is different from your company name, especially if that domain name indicates the value your company brings. Below are examples of domain names:

http://www.yournakedbrand.com/
http://www.basim.co
http://www.eliteperformancenetworking.com/

The extension of your domain should suit your business efforts. If you plan on being broad and international then pick a ".com" or ".co" extension. The domain you pick can impact your growth on traffic, which is why you should make your pick carefully. Sometimes the availability of your preferred domain name may vary, which is why you'll need to make compromises and be creative. To buy your domain, use GoDaddy.com. It is cost effective and the process of pointing your domain to your website is made very simple. When you're purchasing the domain, make sure you keep clicking "No Thanks" to all the up-selling GoDaddy does. Don't let all the stuff they throw at you deviate you from the process of buying the domain name. You shouldn't be paying more than $13 per year for your domain if you make the purchase correctly. Once the purchase is made, be sure to take note of the account number and password so that you can log back in later.

Website-Builders

If you value your time, you'll value a website-builder. There is too much frustration that manifests from having to rely on a developer or an offshore agent to make changes to your website. When you put the responsibility on yourself to make these changes, it becomes a much more productive model. Using the website-builders I recommend below will help you avoid long days of tedious coding. Instead, they provide simple, intuitive, and easy to use platforms to get the direct results you want. We'll be going through a few options that I think make the most sense for building your website. Note that some of the web-builders may offer a free domain with their service. It is still better to purchase the domain separately from GoDaddy to avoid complications in case you end up wanting to switch platforms for building your website down the road.

Getting used to website-builders requires a bit of patience and persistence. Whenever you have to learn something new it is easy to get discouraged. It is crucial that this doesn't happen to you, and that you persevere with the overall objective. Your goal is to build a website using the process I'm sharing with you. Once you've built a real habit behind it, you'll find that on the next occasion it will be much easier and faster. It will become more convenient, and you will find that you have developed a valuable skill. You're learning how to automate the process of web development, and you're also eliminating the entire nuisance behind it. Take advantage of the knowledge I'm sharing with you, it has completely changed my life.

> YOU'RE LEARNING HOW TO AUTOMATE THE PROCESS OF WEB DEVELOPMENT

I used to delegate web work to an offshore team in India. It wasn't long before I realized the process of outsourcing was hurting my profits. The process of having to rely on someone else for my web development kept becoming increasingly stressful. As my business grew further, I felt my website needed to evolve in real time. That need wasn't being fulfilled when I had to rely on someone else to make the changes. I eventually felt the urge to entirely eliminate my dependence on outsourcing and figure out a better way to handle the operations. After much research I carved out a simpler, more effective process to handle web development, and since then I've never looked back.

If you're set on having a custom design then you will have to learn HTML and CSS or hire a web designer. However, if you're just starting out, I would urge you to take the independent route I'm about to guide you though. It is stress-free and you will get the results you're looking for very quickly.

I recommend using one of following website-builders to build your Overnight Website™:

Weebly[1]

The Weebly platform kicks things off with a wide selection of templates that you can adjust and build on. The free version is a great way of getting started as long as you're fine with the small Weebly-branded footer at the bottom of each page. When you upgrade to a premium account you'll be able to create up to ten websites, remove the self-advertising footer they include, increase the amount of server space you're allotted, and have access to a whole variety of new features. The premium costs range from $8-$14 per month depending on the time commitment and payment terms you select. The real advantage of this service comes in its flexibility and ease of use. Once you're up and running, you're able to literally 'drag and drop' content onto your website. If you're keen on the coding part, you have the additional option of editing all the HTML and CSS yourself through the design menu.

Wix[2]

A direct competitor to Weebly, Wix also offers free and premium options. The standard premium

1 http://www.weebly.com/

2 http://www.wix.com/

service is in the same price range as Weebly. The design templates are more tailored towards great aesthetics. The templates are based on HTML5, which gives them a unique look compared to standard websites.

Squarespace[1]

Focused on aesthetics as well, Squarespace has intuitive blogging integration included in their platform. The prices range between $8-$16 depending on the features and upgrades you require. There's a 14-day trial before you are required to make a purchasing decision. Some of the key features that set the platform apart are allowing account sign-ups and setting permission levels. This allows other users to post content and allows you as the administrator to control what actions your users are allowed to perform on your site.

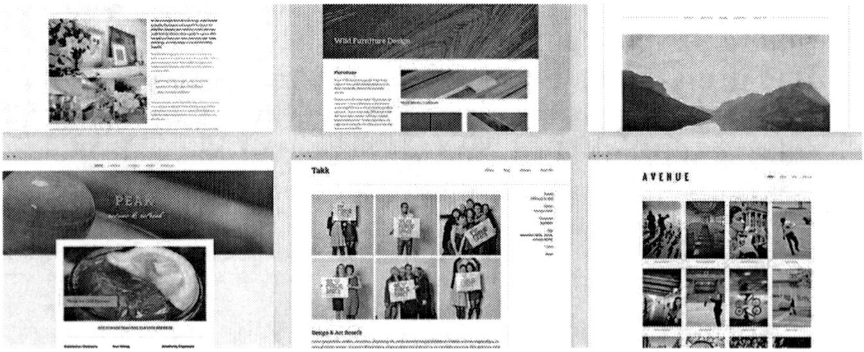

1 http://www.squarespace.com/

Building the Website

As you get used to using a website-builder tool, there are some key things you need to do to make sure you don't lose potential customers. If you're stuck on how to structure it, look at successful examples on the internet for inspiration. Feel free to use http://www.basim.co as a general template to follow. Make sure your site has at least the following sections included:

Website Component	***Utility***
Home	Include all the important information you want your visitors to see right away. First impressions count.
About	Include your story and information about the company.
Products and Services	Outline your products and services along with their descriptions.
Media and Press	If there are any pictures or videos of yourself or your company, include them here. Accumulate press releases or publications about your company here as well.
Contact	Your contact information should be included here. Your prospects should have all the information they need to conveniently reach you.

Website Component	***Utility***
Blog	Connect your blog here. The continually updated content will keep your site fresh. You will learn various blogging options in the next chapter. Even though web-builders provide their own blog creation option, you'll be able to link this section to an external blog as well.

Linking your Domain Name

Once you've picked an appropriate platform for your website, it's just a matter of building it and pointing to it from the domain name that you already purchased through GoDaddy. You can work on your website temporarily through the sub-domain your chosen website-builder gives you for free. However, once your website is complete, you'll want to connect it with the domain you purchased. The process is very similar for most website-builders. In the step-by-step example below, I'll walk you through the process of connecting to your domain on Weebly.

1. Go to settings; indicate what your domain is.

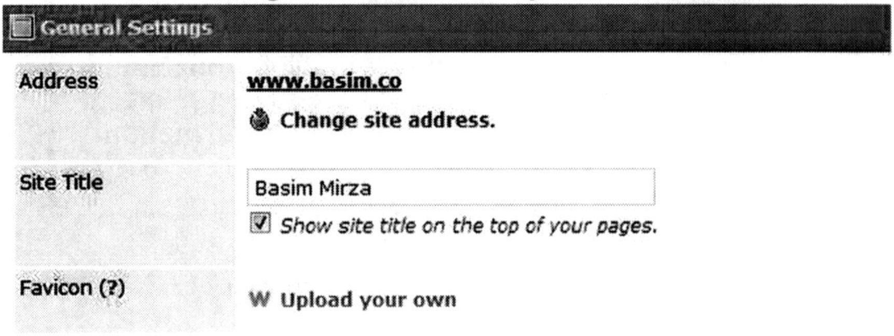

2. Find out what the IP address is for the servers of the platform you're using. If you're having trouble, try searching through the platform's help menu by typing "IP Address" in the search bar.

3. Access your GoDaddy account and enter the control panel for the chosen domain name.

4. Launch the DNS platform for the specified domain.

5. Make sure your "A Records" for "@" and "www" are pointed to the relevant IP Address of your platform. "www" may be originally pointed under the CNAME record. If this is the case, you will have to delete the existing record before pointing it to the new "A Record."

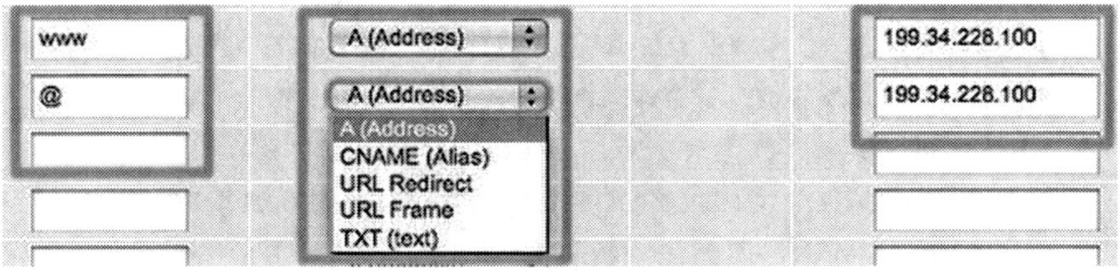

Now it is just a matter of publishing your brand new website and waiting for your domain name to be pointed to the correct location. This process is usually pretty quick. If it takes longer than a few hours then make sure you refresh your cache or try opening the website in a different browser. If you're still unsuccessful then give GoDaddy a call for clarification on what to do.

Overnight Logo™

Building your brand requires a logo to help people recognize your brand structure. However there are much easier, more efficient ways to have your logo made than designing one yourself. The best part about it is that my process will be a fraction of the cost of hiring a designer. I'm really not kidding. If you're new to this personal branding stuff, you should not be paying more than $10 for your logo. Do not let people take advantage of your hard earned money; it is your right to find the best deal in the marketplace. The best option is to use a platform such as Fiverr[1]. You will get an outstanding deal. There are hundreds of people eager to design your logo for $5. I paid only $5 for the "B" Superman logo that's on the front cover of this book. The designer had even sent me 5 other versions and gave me the option to have unlimited revisions. When browsing, explore the reviews and make sure the contractor is credible. You should look for a high number of positive ratings from previous clients, as well as the designer's portfolio.

One Minute Logo

If you really don't have the time, don't have design skills, and you need a custom logo fast, you still have options. You can use the Drawing tool available on Google Drive[2]. This is an effective route because you can save your file as a transparent PNG file, which

1 http://www.fiverr.com/

2 http://drive.google.com/

means you can place the logo on any background. Saving it in other formats would cause a white box to appear, which looks unprofessional. Keep in mind that you can always upgrade your branding and logos when you're able to afford it. The tools I'm demonstrating empower you with the marketing infrastructure required to convert new opportunities.

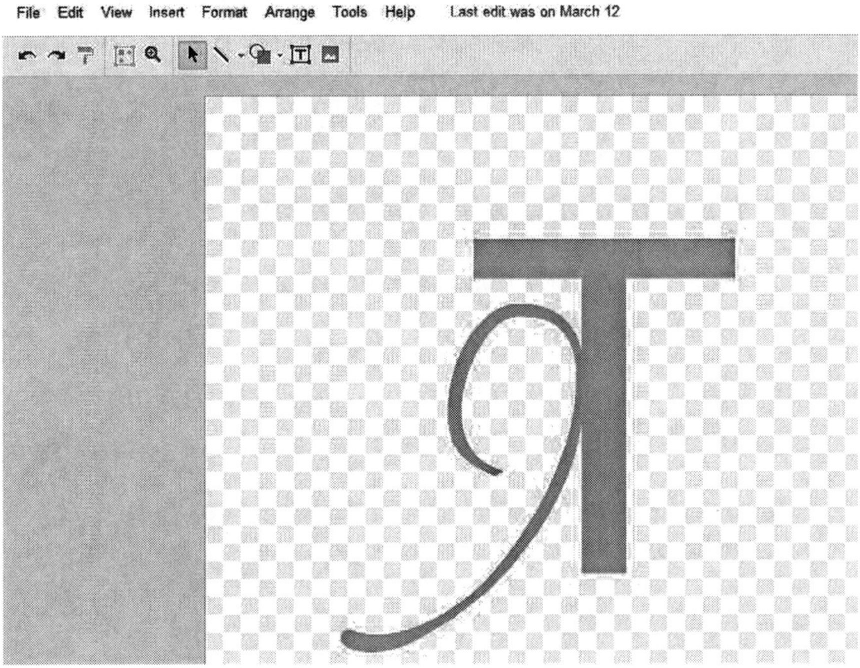

Chapter 4 Checklist

1. *Buy a domain name from GoDaddy.*
2. *Pick a website-builder or alternative solution to build a website.*
3. *Point your domain name to your website and launch it to the internet.*
4. *Have a logo made that is a representation of your brand.*

Chapter 5

Results, Results, Results

Results, no matter how big or small, are the seeds of story telling. Results convey intrinsic value to those engaged with your content and motivate your users by showing them examples of success. Whenever you have results, show them off. The results you have drive the quality of the information you're presenting to your audiences.

Results speak for themselves and are a testament to your success and the happiness you've earned from the work you put in. People want to be a part of something they feel good about. When you give your audience a reason to support you, they *will* support you. Promoting your results creates a sense of exclusivity. This exclusivity drives the value behind your personal brand. Showcasing your results lets the people in your network realize your value. Most people believe in a fair exchange in value. When your audience feels they are receiving value from following your work, they will feel obliged to give back in the form of loyal support. Support can come in the form of marketing, barter, or monetary exchanges. Once you reach the stage of driving intrinsic value through your results, you are in a position to negotiate value with others that require your expertise. This makes your personal brand an engine for profits.

> PROMOTING YOUR RESULTS CREATES A SENSE OF EXCLUSIVITY

Your personal brand eventually becomes an asset that is not only a part of you, but is an entity that always needs to be maintained. The quality of information is directly proportional to the quality of results attained from your line of work. These results are generally a form of success that you've seen. Examples include: landing a business deal, losing 40 pounds, increasing productivity, etc.

Success

It takes time to achieve success. Any result, no matter how big or small, should always be recorded. These small success stories build up to the lifetime stories you want to capture. It builds intrinsic value, and people want to be a part of a good story. Success stories include not just direct results, but the indirect impact on your lifestyle as well. These cause and effect stories demonstrate how your direct results manifest in better overall holistic success and happiness.

Building your success stories takes time and patience, but allows you to reap many benefits and achieve constant positive growth for as long as you're able to maintain your efforts. The key is to not get discouraged and to continue building the right relationships. Give people a reason to support you; let them be intrigued by your success stories. The more focus you're able to add to your passion and business model, the better the results will be. This means you've got to create an infrastructure you can capitalize on. In other words, you've got to do everything you can to come back with the results people want you to achieve. It could be in the form of a lucrative business deal, better health, or even an award. You've got to do whatever it takes to achieve these results and record them. In the following sections, I will first teach you how to add focus to your storytelling, and then I'll help make sure your results are recorded.

Integrating Stories

Finding a way to bring all your work together into a story removes the chaos and simplifies the material for your followers. The ones that want to stay loyal to your personal brand will appreciate creative stories, and tying these stories to your brand will continually build your virtual assets. By using your writing to fill in the gaps between tweets, pictures, and posts, you're able to create a story that makes sense. This process will allow you to build a storyline from scattered information. Use your network to involve content from other individuals in your circle. When people respond to your story, you're building online synergy. It gives people a reason to read your content and leave comments. This engaging approach will also entice people to share your stories with their networks, especially if they've been mentioned and recognized for their expertise.

WHEN PEOPLE RESPOND TO YOUR STORY, YOU'RE BUILDING ONLINE SYNERGY

Building stories out of my results has constantly kept my networks in the loop, no matter where they are located. It has come to a point where my followers anticipate my next move, and show genuine appreciation for what I do. The thank you letters have been fulfilling, and story telling has been a drive for inspiration for me. The process of leading by example not only grabs attention of others, it changes lives. You're able to show what's possible, and build new realities for those around you. Drawing stories from your success will grow your support, and thus traffic to your entire personal brand as well. You will continue to attract new networks, and retain loyalty from current visitors.

Chapter 5 Checklist

1. *Select content that defines professional and/ or personal success (ex. meeting a celebrity, landing a new deal, etc). Writing is effective but capturing a photo as well holds more intrinsic value. Use primarily Facebook to announce new results and use all the other social media tools to promote the post.*

2. *Use Storify to bring your stories together into a weekly story. Summarize some of the key things that have happened and try to bring out content that's relevant to your passions.*

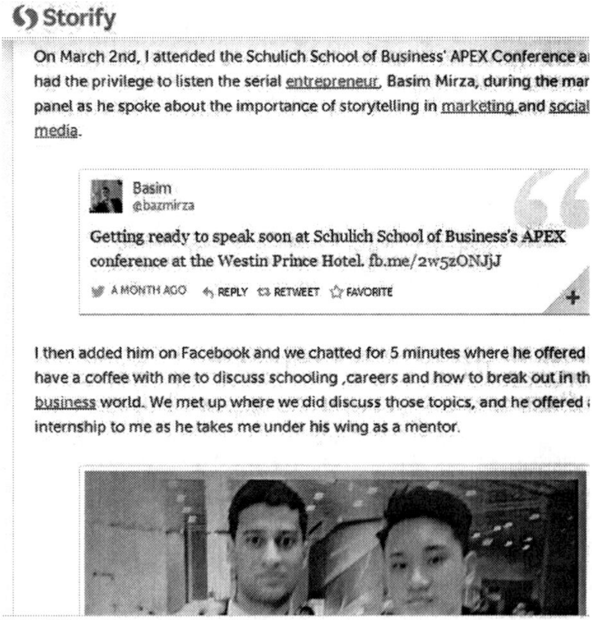

Chapter 6
Building a Community

Every action you take to build your personal brand should also have the aim to build a community. There should be a purpose behind the community that you build and, in a way, it should be what you stand for. Everyone in this community should share the same interests as you and see the value in what you're trying to do. The members of this community will be willing to support you as an individual and learn more about your work. This could include friends and family who are there to support you the most. As you build this community it's your job to stay engaged with it. You are the one that provides the stories, the driving force for unifying your personal community. Your stories create opportunities for interaction amongst the members of your community and, most importantly, create synergy behind what your brand stands for.

FOR PEOPLE TO TAKE YOU SERIOUSLY, IT IS REQUIRED FOR YOU TO ESTABLISH INSTANT TRUST WITH THEM

Penetrating Networks

When I was first exposed to networking, I always thought it was all about meeting as many people as possible. As I devoted more time towards becoming a better networker, I learned that influence is the most effective way to drive value. For people to take you seriously, it is required for you to establish instant trust with them. The best way to accomplish this is to be an influencer at the events you go to. This constantly increases your value, and thus you become more credible. You will find that people will introduce you to others with more emphasis, simply because you have raised your status amongst others. That status will be derived from your influence at such events.

Networking is a big part of promoting yourself and representing the brand that you're building. You should find creative ways to immerse yourself within the right networks and position yourself as the expert within the respected communities. At an event you will have the choice to be one or more of three types of people:

1. *Host: Makes all the arrangements and brings everyone together.*
2. *Influencer: Is a speaker, panelist, sponsor, etc (positioned expert).*
3. *Attendant: Looking to get value out of the event by being there.*

Your priority should always be to either host or influence an event. Although being an attendant is inevitable on many occasions, it's necessary to also be a host or an influencer at enough events as well. This directly raises your value by positioning yourself as someone that demonstrates value by attending any event. As a result, people may feel inclined to give you incentives to attend or speak at their event. By taking this simple yet effective strategy towards networking you're able to build status.

When your brand has perceived value people are willing to negotiate. Event organizers may give you a speaking fee, promote your brand, or give to a charity on your behalf. There are many creative ways to negotiate your value; it's essential that you do so in order to maintain your worth.

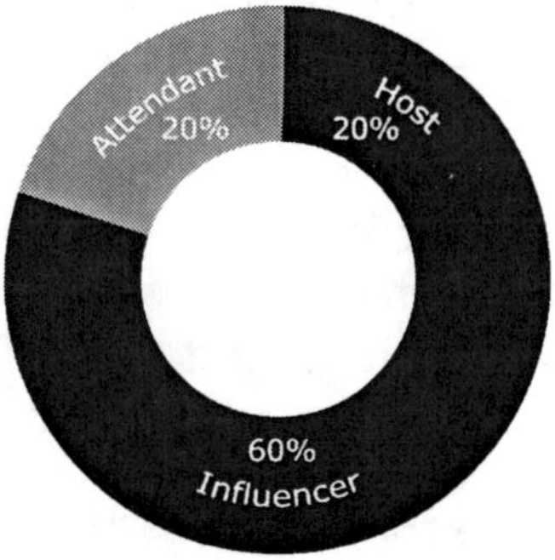

As a rule of thumb you should be spending about 60% of your time on events as an influencer, 20% hosting the right events, and 20% being an attendant. Keep in mind that the events you attend should be high quality and there should be an incentive for you to go. Maintaining high value for your time spent is critical and you should be constantly raising your standards.

Maintaining and Attracting Relationships

There are a number of ways to keep your community robust and full of energy. It is always important to make sure you're engaged. The following simple steps encourage communication and give people a reason to support you:

- Throwing events and parties
- Uploading pictures of you in action
- Promotional giveaways and freebies

- Releasing videos and short updates about your work
- Sharing blog articles, feeds, posts, tweets, etc.

Effective Letters for Business

The following sample letters can be used across all communication platforms ranging from Facebook, LinkedIn, and even classic e-mail. Once you've fully understood how to write certain letters for specific situations, you will have an effective process for networking. Below I've shared with you sample letters that have reaped rewards, and built rapport with my network. Through this style I've managed to develop an effective process for getting results.

Following Up

Hi Bob,

I enjoyed our conversation last week at the golf tournament. I was looking over your LinkedIn profile and was impressed with your credentials. I'm a serial entrepreneur and have been working on multiple projects in your field that may interest you. I would love to meet downtown. Please advise if you're up to meet as well.

Sincerely,

Basim

Pitching to 2nd Degree Network (Friend of a Friend)

Hi Bob,

We're mutually connected through Tom Jones. I

watched your product demo in Singapore (lived there for 10 years, beautiful place). I was very impressed with your platform. I've given talks on social media, and have helped business owners like you generate leads. I've got a unique process that drives results, and adds value. I believe I would make a significant contribution to your bottom line, and for that reason I'd like to meet with you. Please let me know if this interests you.

Thanks,

Basim

Reaching Out to Mutual Links

Hi Bob,

It was recommended that I reach out to you by your colleagues during the recent event. Could we please link up and arrange a time to meet?

Please let me know.

Thanks,

Basim

Introducing Someone

Hi Bob,

I'd like to introduce you to Jane Smith, whom I've CC'd on this email. She expressed interest in a photographer, which led me to writing this introduction. I'd like the both of you to connect and discuss further.

Sincerely,

Basim

Building Strategic Alliances

Leveraging powerful partnerships and finding ways to promote them will build credibility with your target audience. This tactic also creates excellent opportunities for cross-promotion and will help you find new avenues for business growth. Simple media outlets can help spread the word on such strategic alliances. These can come in various forms:

- Press releases, publications, newspapers
- Pictures, videos, marketing materials
- Event marketing and promotional campaigns
- Indication of partnership on website

Take note that you have to be selective when choosing alliances. The relationships have to make sense for both parties. The value proposition should be defined early and both sides should be clear on expectations and outcomes.

Rewarding Relationships

As you grow relationships and build rapport, you might find it helpful to reward loyalty. Giving back to your own community not only makes your followers feel special, it also spreads the right message within your inner circles. It lets people know that you do care about their support and you welcome more of it. You'll hear back from your supporters in meaningful ways by following through on this strategy.

Chapter 6 Checklist:

1. *Evaluate which events you've been to in the past month. Consider restructuring your plan for attending events to honor the ratios outlined in this guide. If you're looking for more "influencer" events, find local events that can help you with public speaking. Toastmasters[1] is a great place to start; they have chapters all over the world. If you are looking for more challenging opportunities then hunt for them. Use persuasion to get on the right panels if necessary. Ask for speaking opportunities. Find ways to host events, even if it means having people over for dinner. Start somewhere so that you get comfortable with hosting events. Eventually you can raise the level of responsibility you're willing to take on.*

2. *Find 3 organizations to build "strategic alliances" with. Find and negotiate the value proposition between both parties. Find multiple ways to engage the working relationships.*

3. *Load up your LinkedIn Network on a social map and develop insights.*

1 http://www.toastmasters.org/

Chapter 7

Simple Search Optimization™

The reason why I coined the term Simple Search Optimization™ (SSO) is because Search Engine Optimization (SEO) does not need to be complicated. I've simplified the process so that not only can you be more effective, you'll also save time and get real results as well. We are in the era of the consumer, and as a consumer you deserve access to the right information. I'm here to break it down for you.

> SEARCH ENGINE OPTIMIZATION DOES NOT NEED TO BE COMPLICATED

Descriptions that Matter

To follow the SSO method you need a Meta Tag description that is simple, concise and contains three key components. The statement should be no more than 25 words. These key components should include:

- Brand Name
  - This could be your personal name, company name, or even the name you've given your website. The name itself is what you will be identified as in the online world so try to keep this consistent for the sake of being found easily through search engines.
- Value proposition
  - What value are you providing to the prospect? Make it clear what your mission

is as a brand and what motivates you. If the statement is consistent with what people are looking for, you'll have more people find you on search engines.

- Location (if applicable)
  - Provide a location if it's relevant to your brand. If you are searching for a job, people may want to know where you are currently located. For a business, it may matter because you could be looking for local clients as well.

Example:

"Basim Mirza is a speaker, author, and a trainer. He helps career and business focused individuals understand the growth potential of their networks, so that they can earn lucrative opportunities."

Keeping Keywords Consistent

Before we dive in to understanding the SSO model, you'll need to understand what your keywords should look like to describe your personal brand and services. These are the specific words someone would use to find you using a search engine. If you are a really good recruiter, you should have keywords like "HR Specialist" in your keywords. Before we understand how to apply these keywords, we will build a list of ten of them. You can always change or add to this list down the road.

Keywords for Soccer Fans	***Keywords for Movie Goers***	***Your Keywords (fill yours out)***
Sports Soccer	Movies	
Soccer betting	Movie reviews	
Soccer	Movie ratings	
Soccer clubs	Movies and dining	
Soccer fans	Movie tickets	
Professional Soccer	Movie theatres	
Soccer players	Movie cinema	
Soccer football	Cinemas	
Soccer items	Movies popcorn	
Soccer gifts	Closest movie theatre	

If you're trying to attract a more local crowd, and location matters to your brand, you can always add the region that is most appropriate to your market before or after each keyword.[1] This would localize the searches for anyone looking for your content within the vicinity you are specifying. Now that you've figured out your brand's keywords, we can move on to the next step.

Optimizing Your Webpage

You will need to make sure the keywords you've picked out for your brand are attached as meta-tags on your website. This shouldn't be a difficult

1 Examples: Calgary, Toronto, Ohio, Canada, China, and Ontario.

process for you. In this guide, I've taken you through the process of using website-builders to build your personal brand into a personal empire. The website-builders I've suggested give you the ability to directly add your Meta Tag keywords and descriptions directly for search engine optimization. When using Weebly, this option is available in the Settings tab. The advanced settings in Weebly allow you to set keywords and descriptions for each page, available under the Pages tab. This allows you to add more keywords and associated descriptions.

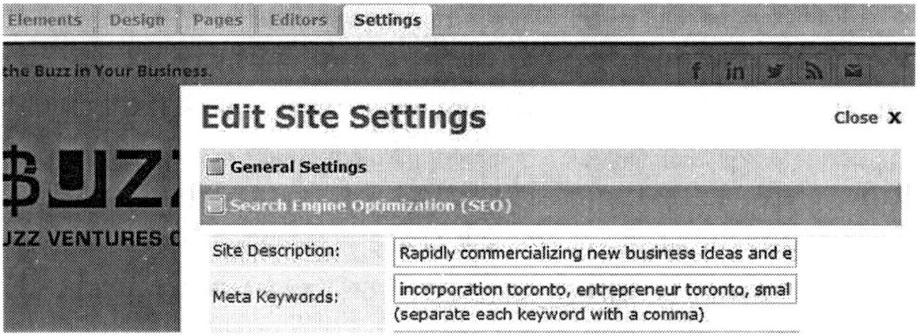

Growing Organic Traffic

Now that we've covered the technical aspects, we can focus on the long-term holistic approach to the SSO model. You've got to identify which web page is helping you convert opportunities. I call this the "Money Page". This could be the page that helps you monetize, land the job you want, or even score a business deal. The page has a purpose, and that purpose is to sell your brand. This is the page you optimize with your Meta Keywords and descriptions.

The promotional entities that surround the Money Page are your social media elements, landing pages, blogs, and directories. We've covered these elements earlier in the guide. However, let's go back and refresh ourselves on the purpose behind each of these elements.

- Social Media: All the media that include your social networks. Your content gets distributed through these platforms and, as a marketer, you emphasize the storytelling aspects behind your brand.
- Landing Pages: These pages integrate your online presence or allow you to differentiate a new marketing channel. As previously discussed, About.me and Eventbrite are examples of platforms that can direct visitors to your Money Page.
- Blogs: Blogs allow you to create and distribute all sorts of multimedia content online. You can position this content to direct traffic towards your Money Page.
- Directories: With directories you're able to advertise certain products and services as a listing. You can point your listings to your Money Page.
- Forums: Many fans and hobbyists engage in discussions through forums. This can be a great way to engage and build rapport with prospects, as well as direct them to your Money Page by inputting direct links.

The Approach to Back-Linking Content

Each channel that's been mentioned above is unique and requires its own approach. You can be creative as long as you input keywords that back-link your content to your website. What this means is that you attach URL links to the keywords you've already built for your Money Page. When trying to post online on a webpage, there's usually a button that looks like a small chain to help you link these keywords. You can't directly link keywords in most social media platforms. However, you can do this on landing pages, directories, forums, and blogs. When you're not able to directly link keywords, make an effort to include them in your content anyways and attach the direct hyperlink to your Money Page. With Twitter and Facebook you could place a hashtag (#) before each keyword. This way followers and prospects will associate your brand to specific keywords. Over time, as you keep following this process, Google will start to take notice of your links and include them in search results. To increase these chances and your effectiveness, make sure you submit your website(s) to the Google search engine.[1]

1 http://www.google.com/submityourcontent/

Simple Search Optimization Model™

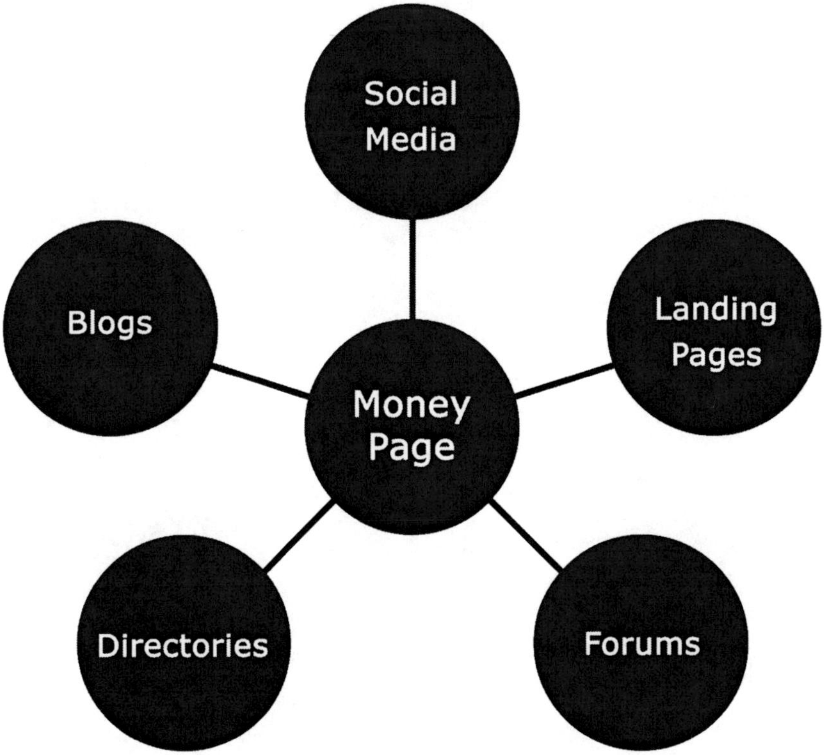

Chapter 8
Rainmaker

Target Market

When planning your lifetime campaign you have to understand what it is you're aiming for. If you don't know who your ideal customer is you will lose focus. This is why it's critical to understand who would buy into your product or services. Even if you don't have a sense of what your products and services are, you need to at least understand what kind of clients you want to do business with. These are your ideal prospects and will be the people reading your blogs, checking out your news feed, or watching your videos. If you're reading this, and you're looking for a job, you should treat your future employer as a prospect or an ideal client. In essence, it's important to understand that you are the CEO of your personal brand. You run the operations and you're the boss of you. These tools are just as applicable to a job seeker as they are to an entrepreneur.

Examples of Passions	***Examples of Ideal Clients***
Athletic Training	*Athletes*
Organic Food	*Executives, Health Enthusiasts*
Social Media	*Business Owners*
Stock Market	*Financial Advisors, Traders*

Having a full understanding of your ideal clients will help you position your content appropriately. The end goal is to monetize and build monetary channels. Through my proven process of building an effective personal brand, you will learn how to build profitable avenues.

Traditional Profits

Throughout this guide I will be referring to two routes for bringing in money: the route of building traditional profits and the monetization route. Through traditional profits, you will establish yourself as an expert and convert better revenues by building your business. With monetization, you will leverage your content to find customers. I've already mentioned that content based on your results builds an excellent personal brand. The next phase is to build a path to direct your target market from your content towards your products or services. You need to create and set up the right channels to make this work. The key here is to not get overwhelmed. Maintain focus on your business objective to build profits. My process of generating new business is non-threatening. You'll be promoting your content instead of your direct business. The content itself will be directed towards converting new customers. Your prospects will be exposed to your expertise without receiving that "he's trying to sell me" vibe that can be a turn-off for some.

> MAINTAIN FOCUS ON YOUR BUSINESS OBJECTIVE TO BUILD PROFITS

Monetization

Monetization is an avenue that brings residual income to the overall business model behind your personal brand. When there is sufficient demand, it creates new channels for monetization. Monetization becomes the art of channeling traffic towards products and services connected to your brand. You're encouraging customers to invest in the tools you're providing as they become more comfortable with your online presence. A combination of an effective process and sufficient demand will drive results in your sales.

Valued Content

Building value behind your online content leads to monetization. The key here is to demonstrate enough value that people in the online world would be happy purchasing access to your exclusive products and services. Your free content should be so damn good that it gives your viewers insight into the incredible value they would receive from your paid content. It is essentially an up-sell, but they should understand the value of what they will potentially be buying.

Affiliates and Online Referrals

As you build your channels for monetization, you may feel enticed to engage support from resellers of your products and services. Affiliates fully rely on reselling your product or service. For this strategy to be impactful you may need to offer the right incentives. Often this means offering higher commission rates. There are a variety of ways to get involved with affiliate marketing. The opportunity may be offered to you through a mutual party you're using to deliver your product or service. Online referrals are a different form of receiving business that relies on trust and partnership. In the online arena, referrals can be tracked through analytics. You can set up online referrals by reaching out to companies that would be willing to promote your product or services in exchange for value. There would have to be an arranged trade-off to make this happen. This trade-off could be monetary or involve cross promotion.

Cost Per Click and AdWords

In the next chapter you'll learn how to identify opportunities through collected metrics and analytics. When you begin to see the traction you're looking for, you'll start to see the opportunities for additional exposure. Pay Per Click (PPC) advertising allows you to directly invest in your online marketing campaigns. The concept is really for generating new leads that would make great clients. If you're willing to invest in your sales leads then this option may make sense. The internet has now made it easier than ever for you to find the right leads for your product or service. Running a PPC campaign allows a platform like Google, Facebook, or YouTube to advertise on your behalf and run ads on webpages viewed by your target market. You pay the advertising platform each time your ad is clicked. That's the cost of your lead. It's important to make sure you have a concrete business model before you engage in a PPC campaign. From the moment your lead clicks your ad to the moment your product is delivered, the engagement with the client needs to be perfect. You don't want your customers to change their mind during the payment process. This is why it is crucial to test your infrastructure before you launch your campaign.

Layered Profits™

> YOUR CLIENTS WILL BE A TESTAMENT TO YOUR BUSINESS MODEL

For your online branding strategies to work effectively you need to think of your operations exactly like running a business. Your clients will be a testament to your business model. The value you provide them will be the source for your content to begin building Layered Profits™. Working at your core business model will allow you to understand the core value proposition you'll be providing on all platforms. This means you're able to utilize new tools to accelerate the process of business building. Once you understand your core business model, you can further extend your brand by servicing accessible clients within your network. This means using your current network to solicit your products and services. The accessible markets are your friends and friends of those friends. These are your first and second degree networks, respectively. They're within your reach and can be reached through direct marketing and promotion. These efforts will be the basis of building your online monetization model. Your entire business model and delivery method needs to be intact before you're able to execute monetization strategies. The additional layer of monetization will capitalize on the success stories already delivered through your traditional efforts and business building.

Layered Profit Model™

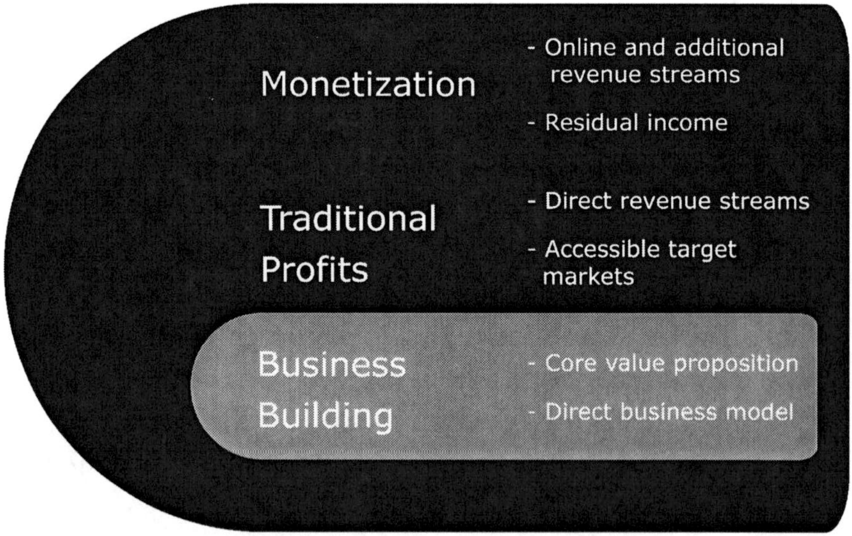

Execution

Once the monetization route is clear, and you know there's opportunity to capitalize, you'll need to develop the right infrastructure to help you fully capitalize on the opportunity. You will know there's a demand when potential clients start asking you for your products or services virtually. It happens when you've developed an online presence to the extent that your prospects are used to having you provide services to them. Now it's just a matter of solidifying your value, because you need to be prepared for when external networks start finding you and asking about your prices. You will need to prepare your infrastructure for this kind of demand. You don't want to be in a position where you have to send potential customers away or make them wait. When your business has reached this point, do whatever it takes to execute.

Channels

The channels you build should streamline the payment process for registering and gaining access to your product. This channel could be in the form of an e-commerce element for a course package if you're licensing your course over the internet for a flat or recurring fee. The process should be smooth and simple for your customers to understand. Whether it's a system you're using or whether you have an accessible PayPal link[1] your customers can use, the payment process should be convenient and reliable.

1 http://www.paypal.com/

Below are some examples of online monetization strategies:

Virtual Consultation

If you're able to convert face-to-face coaching into virtual consultation, you'll save time and money. It directly builds on your online personal brand and allows you to work with clients from all over the world. It takes your coaching career to a new level. All you need is a PayPal link. If someone wants your consultation services online, you just need to set up a timeslot and direct them to the PayPal link to pay your rate. If you're confident your brand is strong, you'll have no problem landing new clients. Once the appointment is made you're able conduct your meeting using online conferencing tools such as Skype[1] or Google Hangouts. There are plenty of other options as well.

[2]

1 http://www.skype.com/

2 Speaking for NSPIRE (http://www.nspire.org/)

Your virtual coaching and mentoring sessions can extend further as you decide to immerse yourself within online communities. You'll engage and learn from others, which will also help you identify what gaps you can improve upon. The online world is a great place to practice, learn, and improve your approach. Not only will it make you a great speaker, you'll also be able to speak with conviction. Your message will carry simply because you'll have a thorough understanding of your field. If you've been video blogging for a few years regularly you'll see a significant difference in your confidence behind the lens. The benefits of engaging online come in many forms. It's important to become fully aware of the tools available to help you get there.

E-commerce Channels

The strategy for creating an online store depends on how secure your brand truly is. You should be able to use your brand to make it easy to sell products online. If your clients already hold intrinsic value in your brand, they'll see value in buying products you recommend. There are different options for building an e-commerce infrastructure. One of the main factors that hold people back is the inability to build the platform. However, if you're able to integrate your shopping cart into your website you will have a more streamlined process for product delivery. The next element to attach to this would be a payment gateway such as PayPal, which is a straightforward integration. Another option, for those that want to fully avoid the costs and time necessary to develop a proprietary platform, is to use a service like Shopify[1]. Shopify allows you to have a readily accessible and easily customizable shopping cart platform. The fees in this case are more expensive, and the service costs more as you build your product base. There are also transactional fees involved when your customers make purchases from your online store.

Getting Paid

When your customer agrees to pay for your product or service, there needs to be a method in place for them to do so. There are plenty of options to make this happen. However, it's very important that you're firm on your value and process. Your clients should be willing to adapt to your process, especially if they are looking to make a change. Time is of the essence when serving clients, which is why your process will make transactions efficient and smooth.

1 http://www.shopify.com/

PayPal is the most commonly used payment gateway for online transactions. There are others but PayPal is certainly the most trusted. There are transactional fees involved, ranging from 1.9% to 4% depending on whether the transactions are international or not. There are other ways to set up your transactional process but take caution as to which service provider you choose. Customers will always prefer a safe and reliable service when it comes to the payment process.

Online Courses

My gradual development of content has transitioned me towards building courses as well. This has become an excellent revenue model because I now have the capabilities to create online programs, and charge for them as well. This allows me to monetize, while also inspiring and motivating others towards success.

Through a strategy of utilizing your current content in addition to creating new content, you're able to build an online curriculum. You can charge for online access to your courses. It's recommended to have some courses available for free so potential customers will get to assess the quality and value of what you're offering. This is also a great strategy to help with up-selling to your paid courses. There are online education platforms such as iTunes

University[1] or Udemy[2] that allow you to license platforms to build your own online education infrastructure. Keep in mind that this takes effort and time. The course content needs to be valuable, you need to go through a qualification process, and you need to make sure there's enough effort spent on building quality footage.

Course Packages

By putting together useful material and packaging them as physical courses in the format of "e-material" could be a way for others to follow a program you've developed. You could also make the courses accessible as Blu-Ray discs or audio files. This builds a variety of outlets from which your material can be purchased.

1 http://www.apple.com/support/itunes-u/

2 http://www.udemy.com/

Electronic File Distribution

The virtual world is becoming an easier and friendlier place for vendors to store files on the cloud before selling them to customers. This can be set up several ways. You can send a downloadable link directly through email upon receiving the payment. Another option would be to use a service such as PayLoads.[1]

E-commerce Structure

Once your brand is established, you should be able to create a stream of products and services directly accessible from your website. Monetization occurs when customers purchase a product through your website. You can directly promote these products and services by leveraging search engine optimization and using Google's range of advertising tools.

Membership Portal and Feed Access

If your fan base sees value in receiving exclusive content from you, put together a membership portal that gives access to such content. You could license current portal technology or build your own. Free services like Pheed[2] allow you to charge people to view your exclusive feeds.

1 http://www.payloadz.com/

2 http://www.pheed.com/

Physical and Virtual Events

Another route for monetization is hosting events. The strength of your brand will help bring in attendants. With this in mind, you need an avenue to convert prospects in to attendants. You can host physical events at specific locations, or even host the events virtually by setting up live video streams through platforms such as Ustream[1] or Google Hangouts. The payment process needs to be simple and straightforward. There also needs to be clear value for the price to attend.

Much of my event planning experience derived from non-profit work and community involvement. When I started an organization called Canada Pakistan Professionals Association[2], I managed to

1 http://www.ustream.tv/

2 http://www.cppa.co/

attract a niche market. Our events sold out very quickly, as our promotional efforts were highly effective. We created an event through the Facebook fan page[1], but also made sure we extensively invited the right networks to the event. This required strong personal brands and influencers to support us. Our first event was held at PwC tower in downtown Toronto. Within 24 hours we sold out at a maximum capacity of 90 people, and had a waiting list of over 100. Our efforts were highly effective. Being able to host successful events such as this allows you build influence amongst your network, as well as create goodwill value.

Cross Promotional Avenues

Understanding the value of your promotional push will help you negotiate the right deals with other businesses looking to market. It needs to be a valuable exchange, however. If it feels like you're doing more for the other party than what they're capable of doing for you, then it may make sense for you to charge a premium. You're providing more value in return, which is why you have sufficient room to negotiate this. It's essential for you to articulate this properly. You can negotiate monetarily or ask for certain perks. Examples of perks could include receiving a certain number of hours of skilled labor, such as video editing or graphic design. By establishing market values you're able to conceptualize a fair deal.

1 http://www.facebook.com/cppa.co/

Public Relations Reach Out

As you build promotional partnerships and new avenues to market your brand, it may seem clear that you need new marketing leverage to spread your content through other channels. There are organizations and companies that won't mind publishing your content on their Facebook Fan Page or as an article on their website. Your traffic will grow significantly when you make an effort to build relationships with such organizations, especially if they have a heavy reach. You will receive new traffic because your link will be included in the post. Organizations that are always looking for content are the ones that will promote you the most, as many of them are community-based organizations. Have the right emails handy for all your PR links. If you want to get a message out to the right people, you could send out an email blast related to specific content you want posted in particular places. Below is a simple email template you can use. Feel free to tweak it to suit your needs.

"Dear Bob,

I've noticed your marketing efforts recently, and I'm really impressed! I would love to find ways to collaborate and engage with your organization. Would you be willing to promote our upcoming events in Toronto? Feel free to check out the website at http://www.websitegoeshere.com where you can find more information. Please advise what works best, and possible next steps.

Sincerely,

Basim Mirza"

Sponsorship and Advertising

> YOUR SPONSORS ARE PAYING CLIENTS THAT WANT ACCESS TO YOUR FAN BASE

Advertising deals can come in the form of both direct and indirect sponsorship. Your sponsors are paying clients that want access to your fan base. The reason for this might be because you share the same target market. By gaining exposure through your promotion, the sponsor will be able to get their name out there. If your business serves customers in a specific location, a direct deal would make complete sense because your target market is shared with other businesses within the same region. There may be other reasons to do a direct deal if there are common interests. It's the preferred way to do business because it cuts out the middleman and you can negotiate freely. An indirect deal involves using affiliates over the internet, or having someone find you an advertising deal. Although these deals could be lucrative, you will need to offer commissions on most of your revenues. Furthermore, this revenue model is getting increasingly competitive. A direct deal will keep the ball in your court, let you stay exclusive, and won't let the market demand fluctuate your value. As you build on this concept, you'll be able to explain the value behind your sponsorship and advertising opportunities by showcasing analytics (covered in the next chapter) and case studies to potential clients. If you are well organized, it becomes an easier sell to pass through corporate budgets for sponsorship.

Chapter 9

Measuring Analytics and Finding Insight

Getting feedback on your efforts through monitoring analytics allows you to regularly improve and evolve your business model towards new opportunities. Statistical measures are getting increasingly precise and will enable you to fully understand the customer demographics you're attracting through your brand.

Tracking Growth

Using analytics will allow you to determine whether you're online presence is growing or not. This becomes clear when you're able to see your viewership. A more important statistic is the number of unique visitors, which ignores any repeat data. Overall, seeing the analytics informs you of whether your viewership is growing. This will let you know whether you're providing the right content to your audience. You can break down the data further and find out what kind of users are looking at your content. This will help you position upcoming content appropriately and, ideally, increase the targeted viewership. This potentially increases your chances of converting revenues through monetization and capitalizing on business leads.

Data for Deals

In the previous chapter we discussed the opportunity for you to leverage your analytical data to find sponsors or advertisers. Setting this up as a presentation can help you get your foot in the door and help you get commitment from the other party.

At the end of the day you need to show what value are you offering potential business partners in terms of potential accessibility to their ideal client. Be sure to know who their ideal client is and how your fan base can support their business model. Once you know the direction to take, setting up the presentation won't be difficult.

Preferred Analytical Tools

Tool	***Utility***	***Purpose***
Google Analytics	Comprehensive analytics retrieved from websites.	Find out key pieces of information about consumer insights. Provides useful information such as unique visits, retention, demographics, location, keywords, etc. Further insight for monetization tools such as AdWords.
Facebook Insights	Comprehensive analytics retrieved from Fan pages.	Understand user behavioral data around a specific promotion. Analytics can be specific to content as well. Virality measures indicates analytics for specific posts.

Tool	***Utility***	***Purpose***
Direct Blog Analytics (Blogger, Tumblr)	Basic analytical data for blogging platforms.	Provides basic information such as unique and general page visits.
YouTube Analytics	Comprehensive and relevant analytics retrieved from your YouTube videos and channel.	Understand user behavior and data behind the video that is relevant, gives further insight on monetization.
HootSuite Analytics	Streamline communication from all Social Media platforms. The analytical part of the platform allows you to build data related to your marketing channels.	The analytical component allows you discover behavioral data from traffic, as well as match responses to preferred keywords.
LinkedIn Analytics	Basic analytics information available to understand profile views and history.	Available with premium option. Could be used to understand how many regular visits your profile is receiving, as well as from which industry, and how people are finding you.

Setting up Analytics

It gets a bit technical to set up the analytics tools you need. However, once you know how to access the data it becomes habitual. Google analytics is the platform that requires the most work. You'll need to take the code they provide you after setting up your account and input it into the HTML of your website(s). Follow the instructions that Google provides you. There are enough additional resources online to help you achieve this. You'll have to wait a few days for the analytics to load, but once they do you're smooth sailing.

Other forms of analytics are available directly from the platforms you use to build your website and blog. However, as mentioned before, they aren't as comprehensive and recognizable as Google Analytics. Other analytics tools available from entities such as YouTube are included automatically; it is just a matter of finding them in the application's menu. You can find the information you're looking for by browsing "Video Manager". You need to have videos uploaded to have access to these features.

Chapter 9 Checklist

1. *Set up analytics for all relevant social media and websites you're using.*

2. *Once the data is being recorded, build a habit of regularly tracking and creating reports. A great way to build presentable reports is to use Microsoft Word and import files and screenshots that point to the relevant information. You can export your reports as PDF documents, which will help you build presentable case studies.*

Chapter 10

Long Term Growth, Residual Value, and Philanthropy

Personal Brand Architecture

Your personal brand stems from everything you present both virtually and physically. Therefore, as you maintain your brand, the infrastructure you've built needs to be consistent with its own branding. How you build your brand matters, but how you present it is crucial as well. Everything you build from scratch should feel consolidated. Your core business model should be present in all the subsets you've built up. The Proctor and Gamble brand does this well with their marketing infrastructure. The company owns a huge portfolio of smaller companies. Recently, they've started presenting the P&G logo more prominently on their portfolio. You can do this tactfully with your personal brand as well. When everything flows your surrounding environment will take notice. This will reflect in the way people perceive your personal brand. You can bring out this brand infrastructure not just in the virtual world, but also in what manifests physically. You represent your brand in the way you dress, talk, and behave. As you create a more integrated personal brand, your life itself will feel more synchronized.

WHEN EVERYTHING FLOWS YOUR SURROUNDING ENVIRONMENT WILL TAKE NOTICE

Maintaining Your Brand

It's necessary to understand that if you neglect your brand, you will neglect your fan base. Once it reaches a point where it's able to sustain itself you can even hire someone to make sure your brand stays up to date. Make sure the person taking care of your brand knows about your specific processes and approaches. He or she will also need to get a sense of what you're brand is all about. By having a long-term approach, you will be able to reap the benefits of having a loyal fan base. This greatly increases the value of your brand and will help you along the way, especially when you try to kick-start new projects. Continue to care for the relationships you've built and find ways to always meet the needs of your followers.

Leadership Presence

As you become more confident with your personal brand, you will come across opportunities to lead. You can breed new leadership by finding emerging talent to take under your wing. These individuals will find ways to help you in return, as your mentorship will hold value in their careers.

Evolving and Seeking Opportunities

Life is all about growing and finding new opportunities. You may be able to break into new territories and find that your business model is evolving. Let this happen, and keep your followers in the loop as well. It shows that you're able to adapt and keep pace. As your personal brand grows, consider building case study documents to present your stories. You may find yourself hired by someone to help him or her get there as well. You might receive coaching opportunities this way, or may be approached for endorsement. Constantly build your brand and add the layers of experience as case study material.

Social Innovation

Having a strong following can help you launch new entities, especially if there's a powerful cause that people are willing to stand behind. Whether you want to build a non-profit, charity, or social start-up, you may find yourself being exposed to new markets. Your initiative will place you in a position of power and the goodwill generated from the extensive work you will need to do will reap rewards for your personal brand and business model.

Idea and Energy

For a great idea to evolve and gain extensive support, you'll need to make sure there are enough opportunities for discussion. The target market that you're looking to gain support from has to be comfortable with the cause. They need to be able to relate to the cause and be willing to stand behind it. For the people that are willing to engage, find ways to collaborate with them towards a focused purpose. Bring in additional support and channel influence from others. The combination of launching a website and building a Facebook group is more than enough to make this happen. First impressions count, and you have to introduce the entire concept the right way to your network if you want them to engage. You have to treat those that you've invited to the network as your members. You have to target people that will be right for the group; they have to have something in common. They could be from the same country, participate in the same event, share the same hobby, etc. You have to make sure there's a strong enough passion when putting effort in to such a venture. Once there's enough virality behind the concept you've created, you can extend the brand further by adding structure. You can appoint new administrators behind the innovation and build an executive infrastructure. Almost instantly you can start serving to the needs of your members, and throw a launch party.

EXTEND THE BRAND FURTHER BY ADDING STRUCTURE

Goodwill

Building non-profit and social innovation companies will pay back in the form of goodwill. Not only are you engaging further with your ideal target market, you're also creating a lasting impression with them. You'll position yourself as a leader in the industry. That can pay you back in immeasurable ways. Situations like these can bring you value in the form of opportunities and relationships.

Conclusion

Having an effective personal brand lands you new opportunities. Whether you're looking for that next promotion, landing a new client, or securing a business deal, your personal brand is an engine for success. You can leverage it to reach new heights and build status amongst your community. Personal branding becomes an asset where you can channel your focus. The output from your focused efforts results in lead generation. We discussed the importance of setting the right infrastructure. Initially it is about setting up your social media platforms, and making sure they're up and running with engaging content. As you build new relationships, you'll have the ability to build rapport. Having effective personal branding strategies will put your relationships on the fast track. Your online presence sets an impression on anyone that wishes to engage with your network. They will feel more inclined to make conversation with you.

Setting up the infrastructure that includes all your social media, blog, website(s), will allow you to launch relationships. However this means that you need to make sure you constantly leverage these tools for effective engagement. This means you also need to stay focused on the purpose behind your personal brand, from which you can record results as seeds for story telling. Use your results to bring awareness, and thus keep your network engaged. They need to feel intrinsically motivated to support you. There are enough distractions in this day and age, which is why you'll have to always be differentiating yourself.

The next steps involve utilizing the architecture that's already there. Continue to build it, and stay on top of upcoming tools that make sense for your personal brand. Just be careful to not pick a tool that wastes your time, there needs to be a return on your investment. Effective tracking and record keeping will help you understand the metrics behind your website and social media; you can relate this to the leads you're converting. The lead conversions are the true measure of your results. Your lead conversion will vary from the other readers of this book, as you may be looking for a particular job, or you may be looking for a business partner. The fact of the matter is that anyone can use this guide to get the results they need. Personal branding is a solution that makes sense, simply because you are investing in yourself as you build it. As you take your infrastructure to the next level, you'll find opportunities to advance what you've built. Take the time to research and explore your avenues, especially if the timing is right. If it makes sense, start delegating work to anyone that is willing to manage what you've established, but do this only when you start to profit. Time and patience is key as you build your personal brand. If you've practiced and executed all the material in this guide, you've already accomplished what most people have yet to figure out. You've persevered, and now it is all about building your personal empire.

YOU ARE INVESTING IN YOURSELF

Glossary

Analytics:

Measurements tools used to analyze online metrics and data related to user behavior.
Example: Google Analytics gives visitor data and metrics for your website.

Back-linking:

Hyper-linking related keywords to the monetized landing page (Money Page).
Example: "Dog Food" on an article hyper-linked to a product website.

Branded Empire:

A marketed infrastructure built to create monetary and goodwill opportunities.
Example: A dog-training expert that is coaching dog owners on how to treat their pets.

Channels (Marketing):

Avenues available or created to help promote or sell a variety of products or services.
Example: Twitter, Facebook, LinkedIn, etc.

Content:

Information relevant to product or services displayed through the internet.
Example: Writing a blog about the importance of new computers.

Cross Promotion:

An agreement between two or more parties to assist each other with marketing and promotion. *Example: Google helps promote YouTube on their search engine.*

Domain:

A link (URL) attached to your website that lets users find you.
Example: http://www.google.com/

E-commerce:

An online shopping infrastructure that sells multiple products and/or services.
Example: E-bay sells thousands of goods and services.

Keywords:

Hyper-linked words placed within content that are directed towards your Money Page.

Landing Page:

A web page used as a separate marketing channel, or as an avenue for promotion.
Example: A golf company creating a specific landing page for their new line of golf clubs.

Layered Profits™:

The concept of prioritizing business building, traditional profits, and online monetization.
Example: Oprah Winfrey built her business from scratch, formed a TV show, and has now built an online element to her content.

Monetization:

The process of building multiple revenue streams from online business operations.
Example: Selling e-commerce products online.

Money Page:

Landing page or website used to convert visitors into paying clients.
Example: A website where you could directly purchase dog food.

Personal Brand:

An individual stamp used to demonstrate expertise to social networks.
Example: Michael Jordan is known as an expert in basketball.

Search Engine Optimization (SEO):

An online marketing model that delivers online traffic growth.

Simple Search Optimization™ (SSO):

An effective and automated back-linking process used to enhance online search visibility and increase traffic.

Unique Visitors:

Analytics data and metrics that doesn't account for repeat visits.

Value Proposition:

What you're able to offer to generate results for others.
Example: Ability to turn regular people into professional athletes.

Website-Builder:

An intuitive tool that simplifies the process of building a website.
Example: Weebly helps you build websites right away.

Resources

http://www.yournakedbrand.com/

http://www.basim.co/

Contact

http://www.basim.co/contact

Final Words

If you made it to this page, you either took the time to read the whole book, or skimmed enough to find it. Either way I owe a big thank you for your interest and support. Getting to the point of writing this page was a challenge, and there was no way I would have ended up here without the support of my close friends and family.

Love,

About the Author

Basim is a speaker, trainer, and an author. He helps career and business focused individuals understand the growth potential of their networks.

Basim has spoken at the renowned Schulich School of Business, which ranks the #1 Business School in the World by Aspen Institute and Wall Street Journal. He's also spoken at University of Toronto, Wilfrid Laurier, and many other established schools across Canada. With the impact and power behind his methodologies, Basim continues to be invited back to speak at these prestigious schools.

He has also been featured as a main speaker for NSPIRE, interviewed by CBC Radio, and has been featured on CityTV, Virgin Radio, and Yahoo Pulse. Basim is extremely passionate about empowering leaders to build their personal brands, and transform them in to personal empires.

Meet Basim and receive free training at

www.basim.co

CPSIA information can be obtained at www.ICGtesting.com
Printed in the USA
LVOW121032200613

339360LV00007B/17/P

9 780984 846276